MORE THAN MOON

MORE THAN MOON

poems by

Jennifer Juneau

Is A Rose Press
2019

Poetry

More Than Moon ©2020 **Jennifer Juneau.** No part of this book
may be reproduced in any manner whatsoever, including electronic,
audio, video, or online formats, without written permission, except
for brief quotations embedded in critical articles and reviews. This
is a literary work. The names, characters, places and incidents are
used as literary devices. Their resemblance, if any, to any real-life
counterparts or actual events is entirely coincidental.

Cover Art: Luminous Sleep, ©2011 Mark Savage
Cover Design: Dale Houstman
Book design and back cover: Jacob Palm

ISBN 978-0-9896245-6-5

Is a Rose Press publishes poetry, experimental writing, hybrid and other work.
We are a cooperative editorial board of writers in the virtual world. Submissions
are by invitation only at this time. Check our website for updates and changes in
this policy.

IsARosePress.com

Is a Rose Press
Minneapolis-Missoula

For Dylan

PART ONE

Ten Photographs of a Life

1.   *baby picture*

I am an exaggeration. A russet leaf swirling under a smoking-cold sun.
Manipulated by a schedule of wind, I settle in a bundle.
I was admired on a branch once. I tried to walk and fell forever into a foxhole.

2.   *childhood portrait*

My days are blotted out. My awkward body so thin. My voice sings like sizzling
chestnuts. A suddenness of Kindergarten guffaws—I am snatched by a hand
that smells like a latchkey. I turn to crumbs in a shifty fist.

3.   *photograph of a volunteer*

I am the gold-crusted hay that beds the baby in the barn. The coarse cloth
of honey that adds flesh to his naked bones. Nourishing and warm. I am sunlit
and taste vague. I overflow to the floor and settle at the foot of a robe.

4.   *wedding picture*

Shapely as blown glass. Clear and unblemished. A succulent lemon. Underneath sequins
my pulp is ripe and good. I am all juice, dispersed in a pellucid pitcher of water
and chunk ice. Granules white and sweet better my flesh. Here, I am in love.

5.   *honeymoon photograph*

I am red humidity. Mosquitoes fester in my ruddy breath. A slow burning coal
prodded by a slice bar. I am the heat of fevers. A pulse convulsing in the a.m.
I crepitate. This is the practice of something new, if only for a bit.

6.   *photograph of a homemaker*

All winter. Staid cold snow woman shaped near a well. I shed cretaceous flakes
when I cry. My orbicular three-part body is snow-white and bitter, bitter-cold.
I think and want coldly. I grope coldly. In pitch I desire bitterly.

7.   *another photograph of a homemaker*

Gunmetal sky, pumice mist. The cobblestone well chokes with my tears in the form
of snow cakes. Snow my floor and walls. Snow my home. I snow. Solitary in snow.
Abstemious in snow. You inside my snow. Night snow black. Crepuscular snow blue.

8.   *bipolar photograph*

Vitiated by undulating sun, my days are moribund. My spotty body turns to corn snow.
My threadbare limbs are ground ice. I seep into flat grass in rivulets as day decides
to go. What have I become?—I have no eyes. I am all screams.

9.   *vacation photo*

I move through ocean grass with the flexibility of a starfish. The water is brackish
and pale green. I scrounge the seafloor of bronze-colored dust. Fetid scent
of crustaceans. I close myself inside a shell. Here I listen to the chatter of pearls.

10.   *future photograph*

Inveterate moss. I have rolled on stones for centuries. I am many greens. I've scaled
castle walls. The ones I've climbed were lined with trees of muscadine. I speak in velvet
tones I speak so slow. A wizened emerald, expensive and wane, I wait for death alone.

Postmodernism

There is a lot to ponder.
What if rain memorizes my address
and becomes my walls and ceiling? Asphalt,
my floor? What if I open my mouth to cry Mary
and it comes out marry, but never merry?
What if when the novel is finished
the paper in the book does not meet
the guidelines for permanence and durability
etc., etc. of the council on Library Resources?

There is a story, rather, was a story, about a little girl
who woke her mother in the middle of the night
(3:00 a.m. to be exact) and said, I'm thirsty.
This happened almost every night in her fourth year.
She wasn't really thirsty, she was saying, I got a fear.
Fear of a dark room that echoes with my voice.
Fear of stretching out my arms only to embrace an empty space.
She deposits that moment into her memory bank
so when she hears the words, I m leaving
you, she'll be familiar with that kind of loneliness. Let's back up.

A little girl is read a fairy tale at bedtime. She does not
remember the hard-pressed maiden winning the hand
of the prince at the end. She dreams of obstacles, foxglove.

The happy ending plummets from the book. She wakes
in a conformation solid as quenched thirst and searches
one empty room after the next for the prince's lullaby.
She'll search for that song the rest of her life
and won't be satisfied until she never finds it.

At Fourteen

"A slew of mopeds
came round our neck

of the woods, high-muck-a-muck
coterie nightly," she said.

How elegantly rich girl whirled
her thick hangout & friends

from her tongue! As if
her skirt of words was to top

my shiftless account of summer:
three local wimps from church group

rolling resin from the flowering tops of hemp,
sharing icebox-pilfered beer & lament

with me & my proximity of blood
as heat wave drove us to blacktop,

grammar school playground our digs for querist
adolescence after dark.

Two-toned twine of events,
woven stoned & plastered on the fringes

of dare & dare not to grow up.
I suppose all towns had'm:

elementary school brick of spies
dividing the privileged from the ruck

to discover, uncover the self. Truth.
Bits of downtown taint, wired on suburban luck.

Defloration

Luna, shall I
compare thee to a day?
A summer's one? A whey-
faced sun bellybloat but spry?

What then? Wayfarer in lunt,
all-girl, marbled pawn.
A pearly Winter sting that pops the raw
red pearl chaliced inside your tight funnel

of flesh?
How trouble solved? The hanger, twisty, sharp & wire.
Hooked mesh

pulls a trick in secret, as sisters
with fingers entwined in discretion conspire.
Salty prawn now gone, in time who will miss her?

Something is Missing, or Amiss

I thought I heard you tiptoeing in.

But it was an early rain

marking each porch step

with its insouciant stain.

Artemis Lost

Anyone—or I—
couldn't tolerate

what was late in arriving.
I squinted to figure out

where you might have been
but darkness disconnected me

from the circumspection
of mankind.

Purblind, I couldn't see the wall
or its grief.

Everyone was asking for you.
I won't forget

the sheen their waiting held
or your absent silhouette.

I would have readily bent
to your celestial frame

had I lent myself to your peerage,
the wolfskin, the beam.

Where was last summer?
The inquisitive eyes of trees?

Where the new moon? The map?
How the attired dream

attracted you like lodestone.
And so you go.

(The headstrong will
won't ground what has wings.)

The cloud drip. The isochromatic shield.
Life is tired. It's true. And triple

triple you

how the arrow cushions reflex.

Where did I put last summer? Under glass?
What dropped

from the slotted sky other than contempt?
A promise maybe. Or a penny.

But nobody can misprize
the indelible gift of light my discoid rival hides.

What You Will Remember After 100 Years' Sleep

is thirst. Not how he looked at first
beside the bed begging for that sticky kiss.
Not what you think you saw
in the face of the shrewd moon above him,
that dear O dear lun-lun-lun-A-tic moon,
what her radiance told you: That it was in my womb
he planted salt. Careful now. Womb?
You're thinking, Wound, and, Salt, and, Mine.
Listen. You are not a sob story.
Forget this room. Remember the spindle
& be glad for the pin-prick. Peel apart
the beaded curtain of rain and step
inside this night. You will find enough drizzle
to quench every detail the story taught you to feel.
Live outside the book and rewrite your own ending.
Sketchy as it may be, it is yours.

Portrait

Her elliptical figure was a mill for technique.
When her sketched body spoke in charcoal
your disdain for beauty was divulged

at your fingertips so that the creative brain in pursuit
of attention nullified brilliance. How blind you are.
Who wouldn't want to flaunt a siren?

Profuse eccentricity is a roughhouse for the eye
and despite how often she sent you scrimmaging
in perplexity for perfection

you returned to the Molotov cocktail that is her assemblage.
What am I compared to this splitch of art?
Ambition meanders with subzero hands,

the under-ripe brow, over-lit,
an uncomely task of erasing shade to make shadow.
Just look at her mouth.

Can aptitude, like water, be held long
before it seeps through the fingers of self-doubt?
What if I spoke with a mouth like that?

A farrago of mud syllables governing the ticket,
your gravy train wrung with smudge, why cling
to the grind of major complacence?

Moist palm, rain-sheared & the homely house
of ransack. She and I had something else in common
other than the umbrage of your fine slack.

I Envy Them, His Mutilated Art

Objects take on different occupations
under the blue studio grass light. By blade & whetstone

multifaceted tackle obscured in a scuttle
of liquid glitz becomes a victim of the stiletto.

The carving of a morning watered down with
prolix rain slobbers over the vicinity

of plate & goblet. What I hold out for him.
My heart thumps as he thrives & sculpts

out a living: a bleating strum-
puppet frazzled from his fray of chipped prizes,

kitsch among the ruins of rainwire.
I tremble in marble gardens

a cool kind of labor-daughter,
clingy in a charitable sense. I assist his half-art,

its leprosy I love,
the abundance, the reckless breakage.

A cracked bust soaked over, glad for a cold snap
bends to the broken lamb deciding its limbs.

The stunted growth of sculpture attempts
to solidify him.

Hurly-burly fragments of cement often lament,
but I praise my elephantine god who outshines all constellations.

Under a convent of stars, let everything break. I'll carry his name,
all flax & floss, & exult in my gain. Marred beauty's loss.

The Light of the Mind, Cold and Planetary

Relinquish a vision?
Wanderlust for word, my task Sisyphean?

Wastrel, you said. I flaw and I flaw,
plummet with the plums.

Fallen fruit from the sage tree of the mind.
Accent, false tense. Dear versicolored friend,

you are mighty in mozzle,
a turncoat in wanion.

Fade and falter, waver and waive
the right to tread hyperopic implosion,

jam of grass. Fair-weather, seasonable thing.
It was only when I died you were pricked

by my invaluable sting.

Moon Song

night blooms, pitchy. if there is a voice out there chanting pithy vespers to
        tranquilize
evening's pixilated mane, clearing its throat to recite, call it by my name.

center my pose under your loaf, dun moon—mother goddess you—like
        sparkling fruit
a vine-ripe bulb of muscadine. i'll shine like a marbled goblet of wine:
        plump & plum
a still, still life

but never, never cumb in your full-bodied light. o, mother, mother moon
 with your glinting skin
materialize out of flotage & brume, unveil the slack masterpiece that i am
minus your gloss.

feed me! am i noth-
ing to you? goddess, you are my life
& i, the gilded progeny
 am an overwrought structure, carved by nature, curved
& nurtured
 a stilted fixture, whim of your stature, i am indebted
to you, would fall to bed—
would wed—would marry you! dazzle me like juliet beseeching

a wary but better-for-it romeo, don't take me slow, make me soon, my
        huntress,
fortuitous moon

bend here, not there, here. render me splendid—but never a fool—here,
nearer
near

Melancholy

Morning plans to unlove itself and day refuses to bloom.
I enter horizontally, an incision in a flattened room
where skylights like oxygen masks stained mulberry

reign above my private mid-hour, my blue cellophane.
Starfire plummets in a hurry: a grazing of bijoux,
a maze of ribbons darkened thickly. And still beauty mends no breakage.

In a pillow's notice a tear-stricken face
shuns the unwelcome visitor in the brain.
I've tried to steer the big picture into another pastime

but morning rose like a slap in the face.
To motor: keep a car's length from my frenzied fulsome
dulled with pain, careworn with scores of patchwork.

Oh no, not your heart, hard as a telephone pole. Listen: that's not rain
tapping tin but the nosedive of a splintering pledge. The crack
in a muscle's valve only saddens the tick. Tomorrow will wizen.

Where to the new embellishment? The replica of bygone lovers
embroils themselves into future embezzlement.
What concludes from a stockpile of grief? Who conspires unmoved?

Wheatfield With Crows

—Vincent van Gogh July 1890; oil on canvas

I find myself returning to it,

its upstroke
feverishly wincing, defying gravity.

Wielded into rows, an intimate sorrow shunts
with each slender spike.

If my eye roams further up

a violent crush of crows
is frozen
into one black swing.

Was it sound? Or did color
petition their wings into a levitating virtuoso?

A viewer's make is only a checkered take
on a fixed landscape

so today I am lit with a measure of vacancy:
I let the landscape consume me,

nourishing its stalks
with my arrival as I veil into the holster

of an infrangible coldness—didn't I?

I couldn't tell the difference
between the missionary and myself

or those frozen birds beating loneliness
out above the stalks.

What foreboding bolstered their trembling?

This field suffers under an immortal civilization.
A destination I can charter.

You Are Not Quickly Moved to Strike

Come. Pretend I am somebody ruth-
less. And to dream that you do, recumbent I'd become
a blonde highbinder (my sigh with a brunette hum
to it) and aim an arrow straight to your soot-

decked affection, but in the end too tired to shoot.
Even if I say, Why not linger, Why not stay?
or, Never go, go as you may
(but do not glance to find me brooding.)

Even trees, thick leaves, leaves in complaint,
in absence of breeze move quicker. Move quick like these.
Move to strike while the iron holds its heat.

What's at stake, if only a game
with someone who somewhat resembles me?
The blonde highbinder, the counterfeit, cutheart thief.

Postcard

Midnight bells to boom & still
the frayed maid sucking up to the moon,
that nefarious stepmum, a fossil
in limbo, sexually frustrated & envious me youth,

nonetheless stunning (after all
she is a woman too) & I am mirrored in her face
alone & sublunary as I am installed
in this glossy rectangular space:

the Alps, phlegmatic & fuliginous
as death, a comely myth this, no prince to smack
my mouth betimes with sublime superficial kiss

or force glass shoe. White flag in wrack,
bent in beam, I scribe to you. Anyone this.
I, my bony shadow. My frick & frack.

In a Stone Room

In a stone room, cold and tomb-like
I'd listen to the gabble of sandpaper tongues.

Catatonic
I'd part the thighs of marbled strangers

and climb enormous hips of cement
with nursery school fingers.

A pervasive world of sculpture
owned my home.

The walls, decked with canvas
wept oil.

The gunmetal stare
of a mother stone and a father stone

beckoned upon hours.
I'd curl into the crook of a glistening elbow.

When I died, they extracted my heart.
It wasn't blue.

My soul took the shape of a hurricane.
After a century passed

white stones lining the path
to the mausoleum darkened like black pearls.

Today no light falls
and nothing has changed

in a stone room.
The gelid world where stones remain.

Wedding

Your bride-to-be wore the face of an assassin,
a foreboding requiring me to skip your wedding.
Instead of New York, I sat all Winter shedding
cynicism in the root of a cold Boston
dormitory. Nothing but mediocre grades, the semester
I moped, secretly hoping you'd phone to say
"Even the greatest men make mistakes." Instead
I learned it's the greatest men who are left to dig
their own messy graves. Had you been stupid
I would have carried you through rain.
But isn't it the clever ones who elect to take the thunder
out of any storm? I am certain you planned to escape.
You did escape. But when that final bullet came, it came
from another direction.

To Endymion

The moon on your breath,
the rape and the riptide.
Seized in sleep, how exquisite you are!
The moon with her sick compulsion
is flamboyant & driven as any sea.

The calendar in motion
makes crows of us.
Time can't pass without mileage;
as youth is shorn we're left with wings
and nestle in our wizened pinions.

But the moon wants no part
of mortality & continues to obsess
over you, pretty one stung in slumber.
The moon on your breath. Stars abiding in trillions.
The perennial rape & the running riptide.

Relic

I've been ruined for years
by the excursions of trespassers.
Once gloss, begrimed.
Once supple, hardened.

A hurricane razed telephone wires
so the town got a couple of men right on it.
Till then, no messages squeaked through
and a drought of stray hearts sought asylum.

I didn't care.
I'm just that gray stone over there or over there.

Conclusion of the Stone Poet

In the end I was anyone's gimcrack stung
and marginalized by moonflaw.
A time I rose like knotgrass in the raw
night, discourse drizzled from my tongue

like allseed fertilizing the unequivocal rent
that divided my ignorance from her light.
Huntress cast a muzzle against my voice again!
(Acumen doesn't come accidental twice.)

I digested her lies, an acrid feast of doom.
Her garden became a sickbay for the wit
as I, monolith in limbo, was a perfect fit
for the jealous nature that characterizes "Moon."

In retrospect I was the chosen bait
for her charade, her false beams to falsify my fate.

PART TWO

An Honored Guest

You were an honored guest at my wedding.
Nobody knew we were lovers
because I was marrying somebody else.
You snipped roses for my cake and slipped me a kiss.

Nobody knew we were lovers
not even the waiters at your French café on East 78th
who snipped roses for anyone's cake, without slipping any kiss.
Dressed to the hilt in my prenuptial blues

the waiters at your French café on East 78th
figured out why I came in alone that night.
Dressed to the hilt in my prenuptial blues
I waited for you to finish work.

I figured out why I came in alone that night:
I knew I was in love with you
waiting for you to finish work.
You must have thought me a fool

to think I was in love with you
because I was marrying somebody else.
You must have thought me a fool
to have you as an honored guest at my wedding.

A Marriage

He asks her to help him
compose a poem.
He wants the words
to sprout long hair
the lines to form eyes
a nose and a mouth
the stanzas to grow breasts, legs
and what's in between them.
He says nothing
about vocal chords or a brain.
This is the way he wants
to keep it. With what he's got
the page will weigh
approximately 115 pounds.
She suggests that flowers bloom
out of breasts, pretty please...
        but he rejects this idea.
He doesn't want a garden, he says
he has no time to tend
or to weed, he just wants to play
inside the poem, formal
as it may be. She asks
if the poem can flip pancakes,
if the poem can clean. Anything!
he says. Except to think.
Or to speak, she reminds him.
Although she knows better.

Mirror Image

From my kitchen window
I can see her.
She resides in a pane of glass.
I watch her flit across her flat
in perfectly timed succession:
first the icebox, then the oven
then she is gone.
I suppose a timer goes off
because she returns to oven
with celerity and finally
apple kuchen.
This ritual continues each day.
I know this woman well—
I imagine it is she who watches me—
she is a halcyon with steadfast eyes
and I, unaware, hovering
over the kitchen sink
elbow deep in inky blue soap.
She studies me, intrigued
by my resolution to household.
She even writes a poem about me,
evaluating my life--the callow wife.
Until one night the light
in her kitchen goes out.
I am left in the dark. A vacation perhaps?
I wait.
I watch and wait
in the interior of my world
while she steps out in the exterior of hers.
Are they not the same?

Home Study

In a dream the social worker came
so I set the house on fire.
She didn't trust me. I tried to explain
that flames are part of a normal home environment
as you stood in the doorway eating a peanut butter
sandwich, nodding in agreement, Yes.
She misjudged us, so you asked for another
agent who had experience with family turbulence.

After she left I was proud of you,
for once you were on my side.
Then you fanned the flames like you used to,
instead of dousing them,
and retreated to an outside world
while I watched from a burning windowpane.

Home Study II

As if home economics
were a film: you beguiled the audience
in the kitchen, capturing the wolf in that fiery pot.

As usual from your plot I emerged unnoticed,
having pushed that wolf down the chimney
on cue. The assemblage applauded.

Not viewing what I did, but viewing only you.

Home Study III

Fealty, kilter
resided in our cottage on the hill.
Rooms allergic to guests.
Nonetheless, a bassinet awaited company.

Floor swept with synergy,
veneer-decorated walls.
And nightly one of us (or you)
paced the vacant halls.

Home Study IV

Bread crowded our pantry.
Crumpled sheets smeared our bed.
Homegrown petals were broken in broken garden rows.
Here, not perfect meant perfect.

For the final home inspection
no subject was taboo, except for the one
about the boyfriend. Who knew last minute
you'd fling him in my direction? Who knew you even knew?

The past landed on our step. I paced the house
wary at what you might say. But your hunger
for bluffing devoured my mistake
where here, perfection was a narrow escape.

Home Study V

The back door slammed in a hurry.
All the yogurt's been eaten, except
for your favorite—blackberry.
The refrigerator's gone on a diet.

The dumbwaiter still vents:
a belly full of dirty silver. I am
the last nickel spent.

Rust bled all over your Fiat
so you flew your airplane instead
while I was kept on autopilot.

Don't bother me!—I'm engaged.
If only to a party line. In the garden
I fished for mint. I can barely slip
into photographs now. Your life seems to fit.

In a Dream

A baby was dead
at the bottom of a swimming pool.
It wasn't our pool
and although it wasn't our baby, we said

we'd love it like a daughter.
Together we blew air into its blue lungs.
She materialized alive and sung
in her own dry bed nursing water.

Ecstatic, we finally had someone to nurture
as she extended a hand in the air.
We built a home for her:

here a table, there a chair.
So much to look forward to! Her need for us grew.
Then suddenly collapsed into the absence which I woke to.

Adoption

You flew to Guatemala to retrieve our second kid,
a task putting devotion to the test.
Not long ago I got rid of arrogance:
the lover I left in Budapest.

I was compelled to become philanthropic
and buy back the girl I was sure I had lost.
Her bronze look, eyes black, no trace
of the blonde hair or fair skin he possessed.

No doubt she was mine. Certain as poverty clung
to the tropical climate of her country I knew
if the river flows it must be a song.
The tune for so long I kept hidden from you.

Starvation

is what separates meat from bone.
She is too skinny, you said.
So I held her to my own breast
as if I were her birth mother. What led

us to nurture a stranger not of our concocted blood
intrigued you. Convinced she took after me,
I confided in her that we were one
of a kind. Spilling formula, you hurried

the plastic bottle into her mouth.
Not for a second would you let
one of us suffer from hunger, nourishing the myth
that Americans are overfed.

Deliberately I let my plate remain bare. I would have
eaten you alive had she not been there.

Insomnia

It's three a.m. and finally to bed, then little one comes to wake me out of
    semi-sleep.
    Mommy, look!—

I walk upstairs and stand and stare: the bathroom is splayed with shit.
    Shit, shit everywhere. In between white tiles,
        walls, in crooks of bookshelves.

At night, like me, he never sleeps.

I put little one in the tub and retreat to my knees.

I want to scream. But don't. Can't. I sit and clean and clean and clean.

    A bloodshot moon watches me through a sky window and this is
    what she sees:
        baby shit, caked in hair, settled beneath fingernails
            like little brown teeth.

I've been up all night! I've been up all night for weeks!

Little one is in the tub laughing. I don't shout. Instead, I opt for the insane
    way out:

    Little one, why are you laughing?
    Do you think this is funny? I am dead tired—
    What if I fall asleep while driving later and die? Huh, little one?
    Your daddy
    Can't take care of you. You'll have to live
    In an orphanage.

Little eyes cry. Big eyes cry too. I'm exhausted...a little bit sick.

Again, to bed. I escape into sleeping pills that won't let me sleep. But make
insomnia tolerable as euphoria swings in waves. Spinning. Spinning.

Little one is not sleepy. I pour a shot glass full of red wine and with my
    thumb
I ladle it messily onto his tongue. Strong grape juice! Nostril-sting. Good

thing.

He's down for the count...heavy lids falling, falling. He's out.

I'm still up waiting, but sleep never comes. I swallow another pill. Hell!—
    I'd
swallow the whole bottle if it weren't for the love of him!

Still nothing...

It's five a.m. and ironically in one hour I'll be in the kitchen to brew coffee.
It's completely dark. The village is as remote as slumber.
Soon odds and ends will fade in here and there,

        here and there

like an old Polaroid assembling themselves into day: one silo. Two fat
        sheep.
Etc., etc. But still I can't sleep,

I can't sleep I can't sleep.

Cleaning House

I was at home with nothing to do, you were at work
and our child in school, so I decided to thoroughly clean
the house.
I began with the refrigerator
 (the size of it kept us thin)
And washed the floor, tapwater dull, then pulled up the carpet
        to vacuum the dirt beneath it.

Cat claws, dead bees left over from the season.

But something wouldn't allow our Hoover upright to swallow it,
        and I found myself on my knees to see.
There, bigger than a breadbox
and more serious than a chair
was an argument we had
                dormant and swollen with rage.

Obstinate thing. Why was it swept there and when?
The evening our son came downstairs, apple juice-thirsty
        and unaware of our feud? So that
distraction wouldn't allow us the luxury to make up?

Recollection broke the detergent-rinsed air, and I felt the warm skin
of another man.

Now you are aloof at the door,
face cold and wet as a stone, and step across the threshold.

Although the house is clean, you're still not home.

Conditioning

Paul Dübel ist mir übel
is sloppily etched on the back of a bench.
Here, at the school playground
German graffiti is sprawled by teenagers.
The only words in English are POT and SEX.
I'm reading between the lines.
My son plays, innocent and four.
High on a jungle gym, nothing more.
He's not thinking about dope or girls.
He runs to me, snags my hand,
but I'm talking to somebody else.
He hurls himself to infinity, he traces the words
written on a slide: *Inge, kann ich nicht ohne dich leben.*
His heart is snug within its chamber
not yet broken by that kind of love.

Distance Lends Enchantment

My fault-finding slid off you
as if throwing grease to Teflon air.
I saw the icky side of romance
and lie here with a difficult heart.
Our home became a time share.

Often enough you tiptoed in
carrying cut-rate love. Stale vinegar
on my tongue. When I said I wanted it all
self-service isn't what I meant.
How easy it would have been

to give you the slip
when the slightest thing you did
sent me into a tailspin.
But I can't volunteer to flee this nest
because frankly, I've been drafted.

So I'll do my time until my time is up.
As for the heart, that sump
brimming with sodden love,
I'll teach it other angles and if all else fails
I'll teach it how to swim.

Tell Tale Heart

You've discovered it was your own heart
beating beneath the floorboards,

a turbo-conundrum propelling you to rip up
each wooden plank

to dismantle the utopia of solitude
only to find your resistance to fall for me was foiled.

Why dress your soapbox in feathers? Why spray-paint
a billboard with your slapdash brainstorm

to vie for my attention when it's simple:
Love is unlatching the shutters of the heart guard.

If homespun schemes were spun haphazardly
botched in cobweb shade, who is to blame?

To admit to love isn't always losing. Why reduce
one failed romance to trichromatic heartbreak?

Sew up the imbroglio that inhabits your better judgment
and let me ache in the neighborhood of what pulses.

Pull the universal language by the roots
and hold me there

so that next time you hear an incessant knocking
it will be mine.

At an October Window

By candlelit prayer
leaves happen. Drizzle-mocked
their incantation like childhood collected
weeping. They creep from tree-bed
all blue-injected
from the blue drugged stomach of moon
and fall, double-spaced
while I stand, single-spaced,
an amen
among day or night. Night.
It's night now, in this dress.
I seem to linger in the same dress forever
dark and pressed like the frock
of a nun. I will

abide until the sky finds itself drunk
in sable and the tide
rises with a different fuse.
A name racing far from something
toward me.

Let autumn keep itself to itself.
Inside, deaf wicks, quick-flamed,
ignite.

Symphony of Myself

An instrument strung in detention.
In word, susurrant.

This composition trembles something
glowing. Shy maybe.

Childlike and ego-wasted.
I conduct a prize-worthy

piece only I heed. Attempt the triolin:
three-stringed melody ablaze.

The confession of a chord
fizzles out the quartet.

Can someone deck out this moment in a tux?
A long glimmering dress?

Comes a generosity in my state-of-the-art
precinct of flux

as I dispatch notes hired by me.
I am the ovation I crave

nightly.
Musical chasm I graze and erupt.

Blitzkreig

I traced a cake of snow
on the windowpane with my finger
mounded it into a ball
and imagined I was God
holding the universe
in my palm.
In the white-heavy night
each leaf-like flake fell
one after another
like insatiable bombs dropping a nation,
wreaking havoc on last year's rose bushes
flattening the flowerbed.
God-like and all
from my fiery heaven of vermillion walls
and Persian rugs
I assumed the role of spectator.
A radiant-white fall-out mounted
enough to drown the neighbor's yard swing
enough to silence a cobblestone well.
Come morning, all greenery will be demolished
and the aftermath of shoveling sidewalks
and skidding through slush-decked streets
will extend its indomitable arms
and seize us.
All thoughts abolished,
I tucked myself inside the safe ribs
of midnight
and dreamt of pale sand
and algid rock
lapping up the sun's multicolored heat.

PART THREE

When Conversation Fails

I've succumbed to the depths of cherrybake:
each word per second juices sour. Runs out.
The retina interprets attraction—but what would it take
to learn your brain? I've entered your world devout

to make this more than just a tumble
in the blind wires of midnight.
Our voices grope for exchange, fumble
cafes, cinema failure. The plight

is to teach me what brings your keen
senses to table. But this humectant rush rages
below the waist of iconic piety, above

resistance. In between, I crave what's in between.
To submerge in the somatic language
we learn to call love.

I Have Always Depended on the Kindness of Strangers

Sister from a vague past
I've come back from farther than that.
Let me in and I'll sing to you the funeral blues.
Why does your skin sweat?
Is this as good at it gets? Do you think
your penury gets a rise out of me?
Let me cross your threshold
chauffeuring mantles of summer fur, a history.

My voice rises above the screech
of a locomotive: I am a revolver
loaded with rhinestones, poems a dead boy wrote.
I wear his tight-lipped melody around my conscience
and it's my choice if I sing it to you in the dark
till darkness finds my voice. It was one trick
after another until they kicked me out of town.
Don't frown—I'm here now
to smother the bruise on your face with a frozen steak.
Your old man's torment hangs in the air about to shriek
and when he finds me here the scene won't be pretty.
So fetch me a drink and kill the lights.
Take a load off sister, this may be a long night.

The Past

It followed us here from New York.
It coveted our territory like a foot soldier.
It found its way in and out of our mouths
and when we thought we could stave it off with views
of the Alps, or bury it in the redolent hem of forest pine,
distract it with ski trips and day trips across the border
to historical villages

it kept turning up in our bed.
Even when we realized discord was here to stay, we acted surprised
when it staggered around our kitchen late at night
with one flick of the light
like a drunk who swallowed shots of our finest kirsch.
No matter how many years we spun into gold or starved
ourselves out of debt, it settled in with us like a bad habit.

Flower

Stopgap in a vase
and stolid as a fragment of wallpaper
your presence generates a voiceless misprision.
After a lover's leave-taking, why did the mood
of an empty room grow cold
under the satellite of your scent?

Silence is footsteps and keys.

Yesterday, scrunched inside the parentheses
of a year, is empty-vesseled and a fib.
But you were chosen for the shearing
by a furnished seduction of canny hands
working discreetly, a long-gone errancy
of a plucking once or otherwise.

If you've never heard the melodious urgency
of a woman's notes rise
 and fall
close to her lover's ear, then how
can you understand my petal-slim keening?

The capsized heart reverses probability
as another loiters in the lives of others.
The quotidian fields, floral and abloom,
absorb sward and sunglaze.
You, not I,
will wither within days.

Spring

Eyes dumb with no love to speak of,
only the heart breaks in the right syllables.
How would you chronicle that then?
Dignity is a pig-headed groom

pining for love at the alter of a season,
but I'm competent enough to croon
for the foolery of two, on standby in a greenroom
waiting for flowers to end: I employ

a claque of dying leaves right on cue
to applaud Spring out of its trite misery.
Spring, Spring, sewn into the meadow
like a trillion billowing buttons yellowing

a riot of stalks. Come split this room
with me. Life is a too, too long script
of floral pleas, a second coming would arrive
in disguise, might be a mightier one, if I were

in need of redundant pungency.
Trees are a rumor ushering in bruised fruit,
the air, punctured with wind chimes
smarts the perfumed apparatus with perfidious tidings.

Winter, Winter, what have you nominated
causing no sentiment or untaught fling?
The fluted crime of greenery pumping a gasket,
uncalled-for, this unabashed impinging.

Solar Eclipse

Two forces slugged it out
in a helix of hours
wrestling for supremacy

in all their dizzy preening
however measly the task seemed
in its ever-changing skein.

Ringed by roses
and intoxicated on floral backtalk
one of them clipped the emptiness they hedged

and held it up to repose
while the other stayed welded
to a windowpane. Composure sank

in its skeletal backache
as the split-
level moon

sounded the blow in its own heady despair.
The air of sky
churned itself inside out.

Sunlight became a cough in the distance
its whereabouts as invisible

as its longing for a world of vivid pigment.
To paint this breakage
into meaning: a portrait of myself over itself.

A fusion to succor a detachment nailed into place
tempering happiness or heartache
like any biddable object lumbering for stability.

Something New

What fell was already rain
before the approximate burst, timing that rare
getaway initiating an attraction that had always been there.
At first you deemed me a "Plain Jane"
and taunted me till you were sure I'd be gone.
Was I the only one in your coterie labeled "maybe?"
Or was I the only one you nicknamed "baby"
in a bed-and-breakfast without any lights on?

At a café in Budapest, across the table
you gazed at me over a cold roast goose.
Your eyes tossed a noose
around my reverie: I, the princess in a fable
the surrounding violins couldn't turn true.
"Stop dreaming," your eyes said, "there are many of you."

Driving it Home and
Keeping it There

My straitlaced drift erased the mark
I had intended. You scoffed at the love song I wrote.
I stood watch: a watch, all boots & a coat
as you left our hotel room unlit & left me in the dark.

If I bottlerocket lines you'd never split
but stay in spite of order or size of font.
For me to be unique all that I want
is a start. An illusionist & fit

I'd pen wet gems you'd strain to see
I'd let love letters rest upon a shelf
disguised as art. Pursuit—does it belie a needful self?
Or does courtship flatter the ego, what does it achieve?

On second thought stay free.
Love scares me.

Vanishing Act

The morning I lost you in Vörösmarty square
I was searching for a pharmacy. Little
did I know you were blending in somewhere
among the musicians and the mimics.
Little did you know I had woken with a flare-
up of morning sickness.
You weren't the type to sport a wedding band
(although I didn't need a husband.)

I found you hidden under a New York Yankees cap.
You took my hand to walk the promenade.
Instead I headed back to our room to take a nap
and make use of the purchase I had made.

As I slept the expecting woman turned the white stick blue.
My inert body's soul was comprised of two.

Next Time We Meet

Next time we meet
it will be at a restaurant
not your place for a take-out mess.
I confess: I'd rather talk

about crooked politicians
than to have sex between the cartons
and the sheets. I'm sick
of indulging you

while listening to other women
send you neon-lit texts.
Besides, I have a voice too
and our affair is overrated.

Next time we meet
we won't be alone. I'll drench myself
in sweet cologne and smolder
in some place you cannot reach.

History Lesson

On an airtight night driving through Berlin late,
unsympathetic to time, your steely eyes were chained
to the road like a mindless factory gate.
I no longer believed in the moon, but what remained
of the black and white prison
you once called home, the past that made you tick.
I strained to understand communism,
your years in the German Democratic Republic.

With a mouth full of flour, even the thickest voice
must tread light.
I loved you more the less I was your choice.

The mess of holes we discovered that night
leaked the plush lawns of my country, though I didn't have all
and all it took to break down your wall.

Then it Came to Me

Even the sun was uncomfortable
the last time we picnicked by the lake,
stale wine and an aging cake
between us. I never realized what stable

meant until I saw a band of nuns
subtracting color from the day.
They had their math straight,
sometimes I wish I had been one,

secure with something constant.
Often I'd miscalculate
the variables, promises you seemed to make
before saying This isn't what I meant.

My mistake. Trying to solve problems too thick
for formulas, a permanent failure at arithmetic.

Sick Love

Black-clouded I hovered over your ego eagerly.
I blew verse into the harrowing day.
But the hammering voices of rain
drove their patter harder & drenched my speech
until rain danced into a hurricane.
My speech was blown out to sea. I was smote into a corner.
My eyes cried Help. Your eyes said, You're on your own!
No, no, Prospero, you ran the show,
whipped up this storm by whim. What didn't I do?
Wasn't it enough that I emptied my dress for you?
Played lover to your self-indulged wreckage.
Played Daughter to your fantastical spastical charms.
I filled my head with books.
I feathered paper with metaphor.
I stroked your long inquisitive beard
with the right answers.
I taught the moon to sing & scintillate
in my (not so) beautiful face.
I mowed these terraqueous grounds
with faithful nods & smiles.
I praised your sunken ship of interrogation
(My verbal love.)

Recreant or rival—you choose.
I dare you to give me something
to really sink my teeth into.

It Lives, It Falls

The tune fell askew and my was sleep upended.
"I miss you," the voice simply said.
As predicted, the jilted lover calls.

Nobody likes to fling their sorrow in the pitch.
On top of that, it's cold out.
Who wouldn't haggle with their sagging heart?

My weary hand slammed the phone on its hook.
"I'm finished with all that," the dream declared, "don't look

back."

The Next Day

Waking long before the alarm went off
I wondered if I heard you in a dream,
if my longing for you was too deep
to ignore. I was half asleep when my cell phone rang Rachmaninoff

and your voice confessed, "It's me."
Rising quickly with my phone pinned to my ear,
barefoot I stumbled out of bed in fear
he'd wake and whispered, 'Let me be."

Unprepared for a guilt trip
I rushed to the kitchen but couldn't shake
your plea, as you the ex-lover in your spurned-ex-lover way
insisted our affair be rekindled:

"You'd realize your mistake if only we could meet."
I thought and then said, "Let me think about it."

Rendezvous

We met at a seedy bratwurst stand
on the outskirts of Munich (you were fatter
than before). For my sake you demanded
we remain discreet. Since when did my life matter?

You lost your wealth and all your girlfriends dumped you.
You considered moving to the south
of France. Wiping mustard from your mouth
I gloated, as you bent the truth.

In the end I wouldn't take you back.
It wasn't because you groveled, or that you lacked
the looks and confidence that once lured
my stupid ass toward you, but because I was bored.

I'll never forget your face as I walked away.
An infuriated child who couldn't have his way.

Your Double

Tired of the mundane, I tried my weekly shopping
in a village far away. With two children in tow
I spied a man who looked exactly like you
(maybe it was you, pompous in your polished shuffle).

Handsome arrogance bled through your pace
sewn into a world knitted by girlfriends.
Nothing has changed.
Clean-shaven—was there a hair out of place?

I couldn't tell—all I knew was even at such
a distance (my hunger absent since last Spring)
I never ached for anyone this much.
Unprepared for epiphanies, I hurried

my restive pack home without purchases.
My curious husband asked, "What did you find?"
"Nothing," I said. Except for what I left behind.
Then changed the subject.

Invisible Love

Were you somebody new to parade in danger?
Or was Spring rebounding in a sick room
inoculating love into unsuspecting strangers?
An ex-love's love for me died with last year's flowers.

Why did I call platonic you at the last minute
to take a walk by the lake? Couldn't I shake
memories of that old lover? Concentrating on his gait—
yes—he was there—and visions of the sun?
His eyes weren't just a fixture
like the lump in my throat that urged me to kiss you.

Surprised, you guided me to a statue
and placed me there to take a picture.
A fine way to distract me: a backdrop of Gottfried Keller
is what saved you. Afterward you said you had to go.

Reluctantly I waved as you left me alone
promising never to call you again in impetuous weather.

Letter Full of Rain

This morning I woke under an awning of awareness
the bearer of illogical precipitation.
If I could explain myself in compounds, must I?
There'd be hundreds of me here dizzying the field

and you wouldn't decipher my babble among the molecules
or innuendos lobbying for requital.
With all this luscious weather trickling down my face
why would I trust happiness? How distant the heart breaks.

You'd accuse me of wasting my youth on dwarfish
fictions anyway. Honesty is a blunt enough lie,
not some phony love letter I can never secure
in your realm of logical reasoning. Passion takes two

so I'm buckling under a permanent brick of supposition.
If only I were a dial that spins time instead, I wouldn't bide
another minute of my day racing toward you,
but to forget you. Even if a reversed clock made you mine.

Fat City

In this corrupt month of smoke and mirror towns
I've purchased a home in the hyper-spoken
section east of Imposterville where one can drown
under false impressions faster than a rainfall of gold.
May I overdose on the eucaine of living
in a mega-wing of my torture castle
and witness what the truly giving
dish and saucer in the arcane kitchens
of hope and prophecy minus one accomplished spin doctor.

I couldn't dream of a life more politic than that
and wouldn't want to bribe any proctor
into solidifying my questionable reputation as fat cat.
On the evening before the pivotal test
I'll sleep well. I'll lick bad history with the best.

Hallowed

Father Confessor
from the stained-glass audience I attend your curtain call.
Thrice you beckon

triply I obey.
Whoever said love like death comes in threes?
My gently lowered head, your kickshaw.

I'd come again if summoned.
I'd collect veinstones with a sudden seriousness.
I've licked my sins clean.

Drunk on purpose, miracle of wine.
Arctic sacristy flushed with frankincense so cold
that it smokes.

Tick my name from your roster
watch it kindle.
I've choked on the body of Christ

our Lord. As it goes wanton one
I wanted none.
In a hushed room, is there no room left to roam?

Like a lost lamb ever often
I break. No matter what version is told,
the story stays old.

Twin

To create the unasked-for
when the world isn't holding its breath
for a pair of quenched roses.

It hurts to look in a mirror. Curled
like an infant, fit to receive death
to retrieve you & me in our linked poses.

Night complements me in a shaky way.
I learn to stay awake in the womb of another
plasma, to swim alone in red salt & sort
out the sopping strings that led to our fate.
Drunk with distress, some voice
phones me at two a.m. to question

my whereabouts, putting me on the spot when I answer.
Soaking cold in a heavy bed. My forehead blotted with fever.

Acknowledgments

Alimentum: "Starvation"; American Poetry Journal: "Spring"; Cimarron Review: "What You Will Remember After 100 Years' Sleep"; Cincinnati Review: "At Fourteen," "Conclusion of the Stone Poet" and "Postcard"; Concho River Review: "The Past,"; Diaphanous Press: "Portrait," "In a Dream," "Symphony of Myself," "Defloration," "Solar Eclipse" and "Something New."; Diner: "A Marriage" and "Insomnia"; DMQ Review: "Melancholy" and "Wheatfield With Crows"; E'ratio: "Distance Lends Enchantment" and "Next Time We Meet"; Falling Star Magazine: "The Next Day" and "Rendezvous" Freefall Magazine: "An Honored Guest"; Innisfree Poetry Journal: "I Have Always Depended on the Kindness of Strangers"; Literary Juice: "Hallowed"; Meat For Tea: "Fat City" Meta/Phor(e)play: "Driving it Home and Keeping it There," "Moon Song" and "Vanishing Act"; Narrative Northeast: "Artemis Lost"; New Writer: "Flower" New Zoo Poetry Review: "Wedding"; Off the Coast: "At an October Window"; Passages North: "Relic" and "Home Study V"; Plainsongs "Sick Love"; Poetry International: "Ten Photographs of a Life"; Poetry Midwest: "Postmodernism"; Poetry Salzburg Review: "Blitzkreig"; Portland Review: "Adoption" and "Home Study"; Prick of the Spindle: "I Envy Them, His Mutilated Art" and "Portrait"; Rio Grande Review: "When Conversation Fails"; Seattle Review: "Mirror Image"; Space and Time Magazine: "Letter Full of Rain"; 2River: "The Light of the Mind, Cold and Planetary"; Untitled, with Passengers: "In a Stone Room"; Yemassee Journal: "Then it Came to Me," "Home Study II," "Home Study III" and "History Lesson"

"Postmodernism" received a prize from the California State Poetry Society

"Spring" was featured on Verse Daily as poem of the day.

"The Light of the Mind, Cold and Planetary" was reprinted in Plath Profiles.

This collection was a finalist in the National Poetry Series.

www.ingramcontent.com/pod-product-compliance
Lightning Source LLC
Chambersburg PA
CBHW020215090426
42734CB00008B/1077